Christ Jesus Provides Blessings for Your Success

Michael Lewis

Copyright © 2020 by Mike Lewis.

ISBN-978-1-6485-8120-5

All rights reserved. No part of this book may be reproduced or transmitted in any form or by any means, electronic or mechanical, including photocopying, recording, or by any information storage and retrieval system, without permission in writing from the copyright owner.

The views expressed in this work are solely those of the author and do not necessarily reflect the views of the publisher, and the publisher hereby disclaims any responsibility for them.

Matchstick Literary
1-888-306-8885
orders@matchliterary.com

Preface

How much faith do you have in our Lord Jesus Christ? How often does He deliver His blessings to you? Do you know that He is near you at all times? I will provide you ways to achieve this.

Congratulations for reading this book!

You must be a special person interested in and committed to blessings. You are among a very fortunate group of blessed people. This book will be helpful in identifying your lifetime focus areas. Jesus can provide a successful way to work on them. He will provide your Christian support.

You have been put on earth for a reason. You have an important purpose to fulfill while here. You have been placed here at this particular time to complete a meaningful task. You were given the knowledge and talents to make it happen.

Lord Christ Jesus can be close by all the time. You can give Him your thoughts and ways. He can be your best friend in life. It's all just waiting for you to claim.

I hope *Christ Jesus Provides Blessings for Your Success* will help you develop action plans for your blessings. Take God's intended steps for achieving His direction. May your blessings be well understood and active in your life forever. May God bless you and reinforce your efforts.

Chapter 1

WHAT IS A BLESSING?

Christ Jesus Provides Blessings for Your Success asks questions that a lot of people have posed. I'm not confident I have all the proper answers to these questions. But I have tried in this book to provide you with some good answers to common questions. However, God provides the blessings, and only He knows all the answers. I hope I have written good questions and possible answers that stimulate your thinking, communication, and planning the execution of your blessings.

"What is a blessing?" is the first question. *Blessings* are unlimited, important, positive things God has provided directly to us. The blessings are both those already received and those yet to come. We only have to believe and exercise our faith in an organized manner to receive the full measure of God's blessings.

God, our heavenly Father, provides for you blessings containing both a natural set of advantages and a set of goals. These blessings are both God-given natural gifts and specific Christian goals for you to achieve. Blessings are important because through them He identifies which of your accomplishments are important to Him and which of your skill areas to use in achieving them. You have already received many of your blessings, but more are yet to come.

Your blessings are in two forms. The first is *nature oriented*. Like you, these blessings are unique. They include things like who your parents are, where you were born and raised, what friends you have been around, what your talents are, how you walk and talk, and many other things God chose for you early in your life. Some basic examples are a unique face, a unique smile, a unique personality, a unique set of intellectual and physical levels of performance, and even a unique heart. God freely gave you these nature-oriented blessings with clear advantages for achievements, and they likely have your attention. You should always remember that you have many nature-oriented blessings and that they were given in the past, are present now (some old and some new), and will likely be available in the future.

A second type of blessing is *goal oriented*. These are Christian goals that God asks you to take action toward and to address the blessings voluntarily due to your beliefs. Most importantly, your blessings involve a unique purpose, a unique set of talents and skills, and a unique *goal-oriented* direction from God. These blessings may include addressing a problem to be solved, maintaining current performance to avoid consequences, serving in a leadership role to provide important support to others with blessing goals, and ensuring more positive actions and desired results. Strong concentration and sincere dedication are needed. You must apply these main requirements to achieve your blessings from God.

The answers provided to questions in this book are not automatic in any way. However, the faith, the dreams, and the positive mind-set from God are especially powerful and the real source of our blessings. Our most common examples are those defined biblically in Matthew 5:1-12 by Jesus for His disciples and a mountain of local people following Him. Some of these blessings are also documented in Luke 6:20-23.

The Matthew and Luke blessingsare identified in the attached "Religion Blessings" section addressed later in this material. In addition to this group of blessings, there are many others that apply to life in today's world. The eight example areas at the end of this book provide a broad range of ideas for modern life issues. You will possibly be reminded of your own particular blessings for which you have a unique purpose and a fixed set of quality characteristics from God to help you achieve them.

You should always carry a positive attitude toward God and His blessings for you. Keep in mind the existence of both your nature-oriented and your goal-oriented blessings and their heavenly source. Your positive attitude will help you to fulfill God's purpose for your life.

Blessed be the God and Father of our Lord Jesus Christ, who has blessed us in Christ with every spiritual blessing in the heavenly places.Ephesians 1:3*Revised Standard Version)*

Chapter 2

WHERE DO BLESSINGS COME FROM AND WHEN?

Special talents (nature-oriented) and good direction (goal-oriented) are blessings coming from God at any place and any point in time He chooses. From the beginning of human civilization, Christians have received and claimed blessings from God to influence the outcomes of their lives. In everyone's minds and hearts, they automatically receive serious performance ideas about many areas of success to be achieved. These beliefs and ideas remain fully recognized in the form of serious blessings from God.

Blessings are based on placing strong attention and feelings about the God-given ideas for performance. After hearing and understanding God's blessings, some individuals have been moved in the right direction at God-determined points in their lives. They have lived successfully as a result of focusing on God-given goals, using natured-oriented talents from God to succeed.

A common characteristic of people who have responded to their blessings is a positive mental attitude about their prospects in life. Positive people have the attitudes and beliefs that they have special talents by God and have a right to achieve good things in life, and they certainly do so.

While some feel blessings are bestowed only on a few fortunate individuals at the right time, the reality is that everyone already has been blessed with special talents and good direction. All that's required is to claim the blessings from God and to learn how to capitalize on them.

For I know the plans I have for you," says the Lord, "plans for welfare and not for evil, to give you a future and a hope.

                  Jeremiah 29:11 *(Revised Standard Version)*

Chapter 3

WHAT IS IMPORTANT ABOUT BLESSINGS?

Blessings are important to you because God has given them to you to execute successfully and generate positive results. You have an important purpose to fulfill while here on earth. Your existence here at this time is not a random event. You have been placed here at a particular location at a certain time to fulfill a blessing by doing a meaningful task.

Some of your blessings are nature oriented and important. Their impact on your life is immediate, and you probably received them when you were a child. You received others later in life to help you fulfill important Christian goals. You may struggle with finding their purposes and with bringing them to completion. You may encounter a variety of circumstances, barriers, and challenges that you have to face head-on and overcome. God will be available to help you understand and succeed.

The extent of your struggles and the degree of your success depend on how you accept your calling and direction from God. You can choose to ignore the calling and to have no success, or you can choose to address the direction from God half-heartedly and find a small measure of success. Or you can enthusiastically tackle the calling and realize a significant degree of success and fulfillment. The choice is completely yours, but in order to satisfy your calling and direction from God, decide to be serious and enthusiastic about your blessings. Fortunately, God has given you the resources and motivation to achieve what He wants to happen in your life.

Focusing on achieving your God-given blessings is very important. You should maintain a mental picture of how well you have achieved some of your goals; however, you also need to concentrate seriously on goals for your current blessings. Sometimes your attention is on special events at special places. For example, your mind focuses on your blessings if you are enjoying something as significant as the Grand Canyon, a mountain sunrise, a seaside sunset, a wedding ceremony, or a newborn child. These provide great inspiration and direct your mind and heart to the importance of your life.

You might feel blessed enough to see a beautiful sunset on a shore like St. John in the US Virgin Islands. (See photo on next page.) However, unless you live on the shore, a vision like that is not required to address your blessings on a daily and weekly basis. You must establish reminders of your blessings, your goals, your plans of action to achieve them, and your level of success. It's important to realize that God is always with you in your daily life and in your normal place of being. God is always present for you, no matter where you are reviewing your blessings.

Sunset on shore at St. John's of theUS Virgin Islands.

May grace and peace be multiplied to you in the knowledge of God and of Jesus our Lord. (***2 Peter 1:2****(Revised Standard Version)*)

Chapter 4

IS IT BENEFICIAL FOR YOU TO ACHIEVE BLESSINGS?

The answer to this question is yes. Christians usually want to achieve their blessings not only for themselves but also for their loved ones, for their communities, and even for society as a whole. However, achievement doesn't always come as easily and as often as it should. Unfortunately, sometimes there are obstacles to overcome.

Like all Christians, you are a special person to God. You have an important purpose: to fulfill your blessings while here on earth. Your existence here on earth at this time is not a random event. You have been placed here at a particular location at a certain time to fulfill meaningful tasks.

You may struggle with finding your purpose and bringing it to completion. You will encounter a variety of circumstances, barriers, and challenges that have to be faced head-on and overcome. The extent of your struggles and the degree of your success depend on how you accept your calling. With your nature-oriented and goal-oriented blessings, you have what it takes to fulfill your blessings, obligations, and goals.

You have a God-given need to be successful and the God-given right to do so. The absolute best this life offers you are the results from blessings being used and the success achieved. God has established the results of blessings existence and achievements that you can enjoy. What He has established for you is beneficial for you to achieve, and it is just waiting for you to claim it.

For God so loved the world that He gave his only Son, that whoever believes in Him should not perish but have eternal life. (John 3:16 *(Revised Standard Version)*

Chapter 5

WHAT'S REQUIRED FOR YOU TO RECEIVE A BLESSING?

You have a God-given right and capability to receive a blessing. The absolute best this life has to offer is in your hands for the taking. You are entitled to a life containing many good things, all of which God has already established for you.

One factor that will have a significant impact on your success is *confidence*. You should be confident in your ability to pursue your calling and be willing to jump in and take it on.

Another factor is *good fortune*. Good fortune has brought some people an overwhelming measure of success; they appear to live charmed lives as they find the outcomes they are called to reap.

A third major factor that will have a significant impact on your success is *knowledge*. Knowledge of what to do, how to do it, and how to keep yourself motivated is critical to achieving your objectives. Profound knowledge will allow you to succeed.

These nature-oriented blessings are key elements for fulfilling your blessings, dreams, goals, and calling. You were meant to achieve major goal-oriented blessings, and you can do so with these three nature-oriented factors and the following affirmations and principles. These are nature-oriented blessings stated from a positive point of view.

- Endowment: God means for you to succeed rather than fail. You are entitled to succeed as long as you pursue a positive, meaningful purpose. Only you can keep yourself from fulfilling your intended purpose.
- Blessings: God has blessed you with assets and talents that have real value. All you have to do to succeed is to learn how to use your assets and talents.
- Positive thinking: If you think you can receive something, you can receive it. If you think positively, you are right. By developing and maintaining positive thinking about your blessing prospects, you can ensure your success.
- Empowerment: Only you have the authority to empower yourself. Only you can give yourself permission and authority to succeed at what you choose to pursue (or at what God has called you to pursue).
- Dreams and goal setting: You can dream whatever you choose to dream and set whatever goals you choose to set for yourself. The dreams you dream and the goals you set are God-given and what you can focus your energies on and move toward. They are the target you establish for your efforts and your life. You can achieve whatever you can meaningfully define, measure, and focus on.
- Persistence and proactivity: Something goes well if you choose to take meaningful action toward your God-given dreams and goals. The more you focus on a target and act on plans to receive it, the more of it you can receive.
- Continual learning: You can succeed with knowledge, which you can obtain by continually learning from each activity, each experience, each success, and each failure.
- Accountability and responsibility: You alone have a desire to pursue your blessing's dreams, goals, and callings. They are yours and yours alone. God put you here on earth at this time to fulfill an important purpose—not just to manage to survive, not to consume precious time and resources, and not to fail at what you have been called to deliver.

May theGod of hope fill you with all joy and peace in believing, so that by the power of the Holy Spirit you may abound in hope. - Romans 15:13

(Revised Standard Version)

Chapter 6

WHAT STEPS NEED TO BE TAKEN?

The "Receiving Your Blessings" Process

There is a process that leads to a plan and results in utilizing nature-oriented blessings while receiving your goal-orientation blessings. It starts with setting goals that pertain to your blessing's execution and accomplishment. Your goals might include achieving a certain level of performance or identifying an important component of your life (nature-oriented blessing). It also may include developing a desired component of life or helping a family member or friend solve a problem or achieve something important to him or her. Or your goals may include other things needing your help. A past blessing that you approached successfully may be a good example for selecting appropriate goals for current blessings.

Next come the development and the documentation of a *vision*, which involves identifying the way you'd like things to turn out. A vision may include things to do that you are comfortable with as well as things that are a challenge for you. The vision helps you identify actions to take and achievements to obtain. After developing the vision, document it and make it available to read so you can pray to God for support in it on a regular basis.

You will then design and document an action plan to identify and carry out the steps needed to execute the vision and achieve your goals. It's kind of like making an important to do list, but your action plan for it will include approaching people or setting aside money.

When you have developed and reviewed an action plan for your selected blessing, review your vision for coordinating and executing the steps of your plan. For reassurance, read the blessing statements, poems, and visions for the different blessing areas at the end of the book. Like your vision, your developed action plan document should be kept in a convenient place where you will see it frequently; this will help motivate you in executing your plan.

If you are serious about claiming your blessing and putting your action plan to work, you should choose to do them in more detail by applying some of the working components below. Before starting the process, some people set aside a specific time each day and each week to work on and review progress on their chosen blessing. The simple step-by-step approach may require only five minutes per day in addition to about ten minutes per week. The sessions involve reviewing your progress, identifying important improvement needed in your approach and skills, and reviewing your action plan's execution. By applying a disciplined approach to these steps, you can likely meet your dreams and goals.

Working Components of the "Receiving Your Blessings" Process

1. Create a set of goals (both measurable and not measurable) to meet your preferred blessing.
2. Define a vision of how your life will be when your blessing is in place.
3. Focus on your blessing with positive affirmations and principles.
4. Create action plans to provide a foundation on which your blessing will work.
5. Execute your action plan on a daily basis.
6. Use an overall measure of success for tracking your blessing as it happens.
7. Use a set of existing and a set of new skills to help you see how much you should improve and how much you are being blessed by God.

The Steps in the "Receiving Your Blessings" Process

And my God will supply every need of yours according to his riches in glory in Christ Jesus.Philippians 4:19*(Revised Standard Version)*

Chapter 7

WHAT CAN YOU GET OUT OF THIS BOOK?

You should receive some direction and motivation to achieve the major goals in your life. You almost certainly have both nature-oriented and goal-oriented blessings from God. Some of your goal-oriented ones have already been achieved; however, you are likely to receive more opportunities.

Addressing your blessings through the recommended approach in this book can give you a combination of happiness, health, longevity, peace, knowledge, skills, wealth, friendship, pride, and love. But most important is the satisfaction received from God, who delivered your blessings.

Make sure you understand your blessings from God, and you are active in them throughout your life. If so, your results will be what you have hoped for. On the following few pages, you will see three helpful God-given influences. Included are an overall "

"Christ Jesus Provides Blessings for Your Success" poem, a diagram of "Receiving Your Blessings" process steps, and a sunset from St. John's shore image. Your existing blessings from God and the new ones you will receive can be successfully claimed and achieved through example tools such as these.

Christ Jesus Provides Blessings for Your Success Poem

You will be blessed to handle good things and also bad strife,
and any challenges to the absolute fullest degree;
You mostly will have many of the good things available in life.
good things that God intended for thee.

May it include many of your days being healthy from beginning to end,
helping your days and years to be nice and long;
May you have some really good skills
and find some important places you belong.

May your life include a true partner and a loving mate
who will always remain at your side,
May your partner support you at the very highest rate
with a complete set of love, harmony, and pride.

May you have enough money to share more than to spend,
with your sharing meeting every important need;
May your faith and patience be serious from now until the end,
often shining through in your life indeed.

May you find fun and adventure every single day
in many things that you do;
May your best examples be available with you to stay,
being an inspiration to the people who know you.

May many of your positive dreams be fulfilled
and some of your highest goals be met;
May God always be near you as you have willed,
and may you never, ever forget.

May you always have some really good friends
who help meet your most challenging needs;
May you always be blessed with contentment from now to the end
in good things planted in you with God's seeds.

The Steps in the "Receiving Your Blessings" Process

Sunset on shore at St. John's of the US Virgin Islands.

Peace I leave with you; my peace I give to you; not as the world gives do I give to you. Let not your hearts be troubled, neither let them be afraid. John 14:27 *(Revised Standard Version)*

Chapter 8

HOW DO YOU ACHIEVE YOUR BLESSINGS THROUGH ACTION PLANS?

You likely have a blessing similar to the blessings listed below. In the following sections, you will find examples of goal-oriented blessings, each with a blessing statement, poem, vision, daily action plan, and weekly action plan. You may want to select one or two to review in order to "steal" some ideas for your own action plans.

- A. Friendship Blessings
- B. Love Blessings
- C. Ambition Blessings
- D. Patience Blessings
- E. Health Blessings
- F. Money Blessings
- G. Fun and Adventure Blessings
- H. Religion Blessings

Come to me, all who labor and are heavy laden, and I will give you rest. Take my yoke upon you, and learn from me; for I am gentle and lowly in heart, and you will find rest for your souls.Matthew 11:28–29*(Revised Standard Version)*

A
Friendship Blessings

Friendship Blessings Statement

May you be blessed with many good friendsthat you seem to find everywhere you go.

May they always support you during good times and badand be willing to simply lend a helping hand or to stand by you in a fight.

May they know you and understand you,loving you and accepting you just the way you are.

May your enemies be few,and may strangers never remain strangers for long.

May your friends always lift you upand never let you down.

May you consistently ask God in prayerto support you in choosing and doing the right thingsto make and keep good friends.

Friendship Blessings Poem

May you be blessed with good friends by the score,
friends on every corner and around every bend,
old friends and new ones, tried, true, and more,
friends who'll be there right up to the end.

May you have friends you can count on whether you lose or win,
friends you can call on whether it is day or night,
friends who'll stick with you during both thick and thin,
friends who'll go to battle with you, no matter the fight.

May you have friendly relationships wherever you may go,
friends who know, understand, love, and accept the real you,
friends ready to say yes and reluctant to say no,
friends who'll support and respect you whatever you do.

May your friends always be available to lend you a hand,
putting you among the first entered on every guest list,
helping you never be lonely and feel left out of the band,
making sure you never will be forgotten and always be missed.

May no friends hold any malice or wish you ill will,
always being in the role of a reliable faithful friend,
one of many who will hang your banner on the highest hill,
allowing any stranger or enemy to vanish with the wind.

May you keep your friends in touch with God in prayer,
having a relationship where He supports them and you all the way,
helping you all to find where to go and what to do there,
Him staying in touch every way every day.

Friendship Blessings Vision

I am making many good new friends, finding them everywhere I go. My old friends remain with me forever.

My friends always work with me to provide meaningful support. They lend a helping hand during good times and bad.

My friends all know me and love me, understanding and accepting me just the way I am.

Many of my enemies, who exist in small numbers, accept my friendship pretty quickly.

My prayers to God acknowledge my friends and their willingness to help me succeed.

Friendship Blessings Process—Daily Action Plan

1. Contact existing friends.
   Examples of things to do: Make telephone calls, send emails, write letters, send cards, or visit.

2. Introduce yourself to new people (potential friends).
   Examples of things to do: Introduce yourself and initiate one-on-one conversations in person (face-to-face), over the phone, or through emails.

3. Do a good deed for someone.
   Examples of things to do: In your "Friendship Blessings" action plan, identify things that allow you to work with and support friends. Help with a task, run an errand, listen to a problem, send flowers or food, offer congratulations on an accomplishment, or give a gift.

Friendship Blessings Process—Weekly Action Plan

1. Review your favorite sections in this book.

2. Study the "Friendship Blessings" section.
   Examples of things to do: Review "Friendship Blessings" statement, poem, vision, and daily action plan.

3. Assess your accomplishments.
   Examples of things to ask: Are you maintaining your close friendships and making new friends? Are you doing good deeds for others? Are you providing support for their problems? Are you celebrating their positive accomplishments?

4. Assess what you've learned.
   Examples of things to ask: What did you accomplish? How many new friends did you make? How many old friends have you had contact with? What improvements in your skills did you achieve? What improvements are needed for next week's plan?

5. Pray to God.
   Examples of things to do: Thank Him for the blessings fresh on your mind. Thank Him for your accomplishments. Ask for His support in next week's plan.

And the peace of God, which passes all understanding, will keep your hearts and your minds in Christ Jesus. Philippians 4:7 *(Revised Standard Version)*

B
Love Blessings

Love BlessingsStatement

Life has no meaning without love.It includes your feelings for all people and animals around you.But first, loving yourself must receive significant attention,followed by others (family, neighbors, friends) who cross your path.

Love is driven by great knowledge and understandingof yourself and all others entering your door of life.Your love relationships with friends are so importantwhen they share what's on their minds and in their hearts.

Love includes your great acceptance and peaceof all characteristics others let you see and understand.These situations produce complete honor and dedication,with love being warm and completely dependable.

You must address and honor a friend's problems.Likewise, you must celebrate their positive results.You must show them your ultimate honor and respect,showing strong concern and admiration for all they experience.

You must react well to all that's positively said and doneand adjust to all that is silently kept in their hearts.Love is greatly heartfelt and special,creating positive feelings, smiles, laughs, and tears.

Love for others produces significant trust and complete forgiveness,with gifts received by others as well as yourself.Love is no doubt based on very important God-given blessings,so it should be strongly emphasized in your thoughts and prayers.

Love Blessings Poem

Love provides great knowledge and understanding
of who you are and who you live to be;
Love includes great acceptance and peace handing,
because of all the characteristics your friends let you see.

Love is based on complete honor and dedicated will
to making everything in your relationships right;
Love is being completely dependable still
during every day and every night.

Love is accepting others' problems, having a good effect,
and reacting to successes with positive attention and cheer;
Love is giving the ultimate honor and highest respect,
showing to others admiration strong and clear.

Love is always responding positive and strong,
to everything your friends have said and done;
Love is greatly heartfelt, special, deep, and long,
while wonderful feelings, smiles, and tears have won.

Love is significant forgiveness and complete trust
received by others, as well as your own.;
Love is fantastically recognized blessings with no dirt and dust,
enhanced by prayer with warm love characteristics never gone.

Love Blessings Vision

I am blessed with a great feeling of love,
I'm sharing it strongly with a large number of love friends;
    Included are my spouse, family, neighbors, church members,
    fellow workers, friends, and acquaintances.

We share all our important problems and successes.
    We identify ways that we can help solve
    problems and celebrate successes.

    I have followed through on the important things
    we have identified that will help my friends;
They fully appreciate what I have accomplished for them.

This has helped bring to my love friends some self-acceptance,
    positive thinking, forgiveness, peace, and honor;
    It has brought them plenty of positive feelings
        that result in laughter, smiles, and tears.

    I have had a good number of contacts
        with friends who need my love;
Helping improve my friends' feelings and executing my
action plan have brought me self-confidence, self-acceptance,
    joy, respect, positive relationships, and closeness to God.

Love Blessings Process—Daily Action Plan

1. Read the "Love Blessings" sections.
   Examples of things to do: Recall the progress you made on this yesterday. Mentally lay out your plan for achieving the vision today.

2. Contact some friends you love.
   Examples of things to do: Make telephone calls, send emails, write letters, send cards, or visit.

3. Ask how their situation in life is.
   Examples of things to ask: How are you doing? How are those situations you have told me about? What's going on in your life today? Where are you headed now?

4. Provide any support they need.
   Examples of things to do: Make sure you understand their problems. Offer to help however they need support. Make sure you understand their successes. Offer to help celebrate significant happenings.

5. Look back on your day and evaluate.
   Examples of ways to improve: Assess how many loved ones you have made contact with today. Evaluate how well you have offered to support them. If your plan for helping them is not sufficient, contact them and offer better plans.

Love Blessings Process—Weekly Action Plan

1. Review your favorite sections in this book.

2. Study the "Love Blessings" section.
   Examples of things to do: Review "Love Blessings" statement, poem, vision, and daily action plan.

3. Assess your accomplishments.
   Examples of things to do: Count the friends who have said they love you. Count the number of friends you have forgiven who have also forgiven you. Count the friends who have supported you when you had a problem. Count the celebrations of positive accomplishments.

4. Assess what you've learned.
   Examples of things to ask: What did you accomplish? What improvements in your skills did you achieve? What improvements are needed for the next week's plan? What plans do you have to ensure love with all your friends?

5. Pray to God.
   Examples of things to do: Thank Him for the blessings fresh on your mind. Thank Him for your accomplishments. Ask for His support in next week's plan.

Blessed are the poor in spirit, for theirs is the kingdom of heaven.

Matthew 5:3
(Revised Standard Version)

C
Ambition Blessings

Ambition Blessings Statement

You must have ambition blessings before you can get anywhere.God has provided blessings for ambition to you,including setting directions, goals, and plans for all types of blessings;This involves reviewing all your key blessings and for each establishing the vision, goals, and action plan based on your leadership skills.

Successful ambition includes leadership skills and application.This includes learning, development, and high performance,Involved is the ongoing improvement of action plans, friendships, and personal skills;This improvement will involve an ongoing understanding of execution opportunities and requirements to make progress on your blessings.

An execution strategy is very important in meeting blessing requirements. High-quality friendships should be included in plans for high-level ambitions;The quality of your friendships and yourself will definitely make a huge difference.After including friends in a plan to achieve a blessing, it's very important to provide strategic understanding
to them and share your love to get them going.

Your help to your participating friends is critical.If they struggle executing their roles, you must apply your love blessings and friendship blessings to help execute the plan;This involves meeting often to review their progress and giving as much positive feedback as possible.

To maximize ambition blessings, communicate your role, your determination, and your progress, and pray to God as often as possible.

Ambition Blessings Poem

For success, God gives an ambition blessing for each of us.
You must have it and apply it to get anything anywhere;
You must be ambitious on your action plans
to avoid a commitment fuss,
using some basic leadership skills that you can bear.

Ambitiously applying some leadership skills can be intimidating,
but you need only use them on basic project
actions you understand and know.
It is important for making improvements in your rating of
action plans, friends' awareness, and personal skills as you go.

You must use a strategic plan to meet all blessing needs.
High project achievement needs high-quality plans
and high-quality friendships as well;
Communicating fully with friends is a very important deed,
and sharing love with friends is even more important, I can tell.

Using ambition for love and friendship on
participants, you will become succeeded.
It's so critical to the execution of the plan.
Listening to their reaction to their involvement is needed,
but so is praying to God, the real leader, as best as you can.

Ambition Blessings Vision

I am using ambition blessings from Godfor my success;I have addressed them in an ambitious wayand am successful in most all that I do.

I have logically set strategies and action plansfor each one of my other blessings;And to be as successful as I desire,I have used some basic leadership skills as well as action plans for love and friendship.

Leadership responsibility is sometimes intimidating.I only apply it to basic, important actionsused on my projects;I am making improvements as needed to action plans,
friends' awareness, and my personal skills.

My blessings action plans are strategically designed
for high-level projects, which include high-
quality plans and high-quality friendships;I communicate well with friends
and share love with them as well.

I apply the love and friendship blessingsto plan participants,I see critical results from the execution of the plan;I also successfully pray to God,who is the real leader of all that I do.

Ambition Blessings Process—Daily Action Plan

1. Read the "Ambition Blessings" section.
   Examples of things to do: Recall the progress you made on this yesterday. Strategically lay out your plan for achieving the vision today.

2. Contact some friends you work with on your ambition blessings.
   Examples of things to do: Follow the ambition blessings approach for contacting friends. Make telephone calls, send emails, write letters, send cards, or visit. Measure the existing friends you contacted.

3. Ask your friends how their situation is in life and on projects.
   Examples of things to ask: How are you doing? How are those situations you have told me about? What's going on in your life and our joint projects today? Where are you headed now?

4. Provide any support they need.
   Examples of things to do: Make sure you understand friends' problems. Offer to help however they need support. Make sure you understand their successes. Offer to help celebrate significant positive happenings.

5. Look back on your day and evaluate.
   Examples of ways to improve: Assess how much leadership you have applied today. Evaluate how well you have offered to support the team. If your plan for working with them is not sufficient, contact them and offer a better plan.

Ambition Blessings Process—Weekly Action Plan

1. Review your favorite sections in this book.

2. Study the "Ambition Blessings" section.
   Examples of things to do: Concentrate on the "Ambition Blessings' statement, poem, vision, and daily action plan.

3. Assess your friends' accomplishments.
   Examples of things to do: Provide some support for your friends. Celebrate their positive accomplishments. Measure the number of problems you and your friends are working on. Measure the number of your problems you and your friends have dealt with together and solved.

4. Assess what you've learned.
   Examples of things to ask: Ask what did you accomplish? What improvements in your skills did you achieve? What improvements are needed for the next week's plan?

5. Pray to God.
   Examples of things to do: Thank Him for the blessings fresh in your mind. Thank Him for your accomplishments and those of your friends. Ask for His support in next week's plan.

Blessed are those who mourn, for they shall be comforted. Matthew 5:4 *(Revised Standard Version)*

D
Patience Blessings

Patience Blessings Statement

May you be blessed with patience, emotional control, and peace of mind. May you always be tolerant of others and their faults.

May you not get angry or irritated easily. May you never lose control and lash out at others (especially family and friends).

May your first reaction to an error or misdeed by another personbe to patiently confront, discuss, and counsel on how to address the issue.

May you always focus on important priorities, the big picture, and long-range goals. May you maintain a feeling of quiet confidence and peace until an endeavor comes to its successful completion.

When your endeavors fail to end in meeting your desired goals, meet the situation with a smile and focus on learning from the experience.

May you thoroughly enjoy working with people and teams on projects. Laugh a lot, and gain strength and energy from the experience.

May you have a minimum of pet peeves. Allow nothing to overcome your patience and your ability to get along with others.

May you be confident with yourself and your capabilities. May you be a good team player, leader, and coach.

May you love your family and friends and all interactions with them. Ask God in prayer to support you in being patient in all situations.

Patience Blessings Poem

May friends be your constant companions in every action, word, and deed.
May you always treat kindly the faults of others that you find.
May patience be your trademark and acceptance be your creed.
May patience in your heart bring peace and contentment to your mind.

May you never lash out at another's unintended error or wrong.
May you be hard to anger but quick to agree.
May you offer support and a wish to be strong.
May you never lose control such that others might see.

May you focus on what's important and keep your perspective in line, when any endeavor fails to land squarely on the mark.
May you maintain a quiet confidence that things will work out just fine.
May you always face it with a smile and be ready to reembark.

May nothing test your patience, and may your pet peeves be few.
May you always be calm when working with people in large groups and small.
May you always understand others as you would have them understand you.
May you provide a cheerful attitude that provides strength and energy to all.

May you accept all things needing to be addressed with calm sense.
May your patience stay straight and never bent.
May you apply all your personal skills to cross over the impatience fence.
May you pray to God for His support for patience among all other blessings He has sent.

Patience Blessings Vision

I usually have patience, emotional control, peace of mind, and tolerance of others (including family and friends) and their faults.

I never get angry or aggravated easily, losing control and lashing out at others. I patiently confront, discuss, and counsel on how to address an issue when a family member or friend makes an error or does a misdeed.

I have used my patience to establish important priorities, the big picture, and long-range goals. I use patience to receive a feeling of quiet confidence and peace of mind.
In these cases, I receive successful completion of projects.

I operate on projects with a smile and focus on learning from the experience. I allow nothing to overcome my patience and my ability to get along with others. I laugh a lot and gain strength and energy with friends and teams.

I am confident in myself and my capabilities. I am a good team player, leader, and coach, and I love family members and friends and all my interactions with them.

I receive comfort and motivation to improve every time I pray to God about my patience blessings projects and efforts.

Patience Blessings Process—Daily Action Plan

1. Control my temper.
   Examples of situations to handle without blowing up: Count the times I haven't had patience with family members (spouse, child, parent, brother, sister), at work (boss, coworker, employee, team, customer), at school (student, teacher), with other individuals (friend, neighbor, motorist), with groups (church, government officials), with pets, and with things (appliance, tool, vehicle).

2. Display my maturity and acceptance.
   Examples of things to do: Count the hours or the percentage of time I have been able to remain calm, let a problem pass, confront issues, discuss issues with the source (friend), counsel the source, solve the problem, or remain friendly.

Patience Blessings Process—Weekly Action Plan

1. Review your favorite sections in this book.

2. Study the "Patience Blessings" section.
    Examples of things to do: Review "Patience Blessings" statement, poem, vision, and daily action plan.

3. Assess your accomplishments.
    Examples of things to do: Keep track of the number of your mature responses to difficult or negative situations you faced and had to handle.

4. Address your problems.
    Examples of things to do: Count the times you have been able to avoid blow-ups with yourself, family, friends, church members, coworkers, school kids and staff, other people, and pets. Remain calm. Let it pass.

5. Assess what you've learned.
    Examples of things to do: Review problems you handled or didn't handle. What did you accomplish? For example, did you remain calm, let it pass, confront the issue, discuss the issue, counsel the source, solve problems, or remain friends? What improvements in your skills did you achieve? What improvements are needed for the next week's plan?

6. Pray to God.
    Examples of things to do: Thank Him for all the blessings fresh on your mind (including patience blessings). Thank Him for your accomplishments. Ask for His support in next week's plan.

Blessed are the meek, for they shall inherit the earth.
Matthew 5:5 *(Revised Standard Version)*

E
Health Blessings

Health Blessings Statement

May you be blessed with health and well-being, allowing you to enjoy life to the fullest.

May your body always perform as it was intended, responding to every physical challenge your activities present to it.

May you always feel healthy and ready to perform, being full of energy and free of illness and pain.

May you always feel strong, capable, and ready to perform, plunging into every endeavor with vigor and enthusiasm.

May you look and feel fit and trim, never feeling old but forever young.

May you live a long, active, healthy, and productive life, increasing joy and satisfaction to be fully able to enjoy each phase of life.

May you apply good health standards to everything you do, praying to God for your health and feeling great every day.

Health Blessings Poem

May you be blessed with well-being and health.
May your body always perform as it was intended.
May your vitality be a major source of personal wealth,
responding to every physical challenge without needing to be mended.

May you always feel strong, capable, and steady.
May you always feel healthy and ready to go.
May you plunge into life with a heart willing, able, and ready,
being full of energy and free of illness, pain, and woe.

May you look and feel firm, fit, and trim,
checking on scales and in a mirror everyday.
May you never feel old but forever young with vigor and vim,
always feeling positive and committed to health along the way.

May you enjoy your life to the fullest of measures.
May you achieve great health from everything you do.
May you tackle each phase with increasing joy, satisfaction, and pleasures,
praying that God helps bring a great health standard for you.

Health Blessings Vision

I am consistently working to achieve good health and well-being.

I execute a well-designed exercise program, keeping my body in good shape. I have a close friend do it with me, helping me to build good motivation and love.

I am full of energy and free of illness and pain. I always feel strong, capable, and ready, following my blessing plans with vigor and enthusiasm.

I achieve this by using a strong combination of getting enough sleep, eating the right foods, drinking lots of water, walking, running, exercising, playing sports, and relaxing.

I avoid unhealthy behaviors, such as consuming too much sugar, caffeine, fat, and junk food,
I never smoke, use excessive alcohol, abuse drugs, or watch too much TV.

I love the way my appearance has improved;
I am looking fit and trim and feeling younger. I am living an active, healthy, and productive life, increasing my joy and satisfaction.

I pray every day to God to support me in following this vision, feeling I will live forever in good health.

Health Blessings Process—Daily Action Plan

1. Add good, healthy habits.
   Examples of things to do: get enough sleep, eat a variety of healthy foods, drink lots of water, walk instead of ride, exercise, participate in sports, and do relaxation exercises.

2. Avoid or break bad, unhealthy habits.
   Examples of things to avoid: eating too much sugar, drinking too much caffeine, eating fatty junk foods, overeating, smoking, consuming excessive alcohol, using drugs, watching too much TV.

Health Blessings Process—Weekly Action Plan

1. Review your favorite sections in this book.

2. Study the "Physical Blessings" section.
    Examples of things to do: "Physical Blessings" statement, poem, vision, and daily action plan.

3. Assess your accomplishments.
    Examples of things to do: Do good and healthy things (e.g., get enough sleep, eat the right foods, drink lots of water, walk, exercise, play sports, and relax). Assess the number of physical exercises you do and the number of days you follow a healthy diet.

4. Address your problems.
    Examples of things to do: Avoid unhealthy behaviors, such as too much sugar, too much caffeine, too much fat and junk food, overeating, smoking, excessive alcohol or drug use, and too much TV).

5. Assess what you've learned.
    Examples of things to ask: What did you accomplish? Did you do good and healthy things? (See number 3 above.) Did you avoid unhealthy behaviors? (See number 4 above.) What improvements in your skills and habits did you achieve? What improvements are needed for the next week's plan?

6. Pray to God.
    Examples of things to do: Thank Him for all the blessings fresh on your mind (including health blessings). Thank Him for your accomplishments. Ask for His support in next week's plan.

Blessed are those who hunger and thirst for righteousness, for they shall be satisfied. Matthew 5:6 *(Revised Standard Version)*

F
Money Blessings

Money Blessings Statement

May you be able to live comfortably and happily within your means and to cover the financial needs of your blessings.

May you be blessed with a monetary gift from God for meeting important family needs, helping solve friends' problems, and donating money for the needy.

May each and every one of your financial ventures yield a positive cash flow, leaving you more financially secure for yourself and everyone you know in need.

May you be able to easily afford for your family the basic necessities and slim luxuries that life has to offer, keeping you comfortable and happy the rest of your life.

May you buy everything you need to support your family and donate funds so that you never want to spend otherwise.

May you have to work less and less to produce enough income, finding that you have more time and resources to focus on your blessings.

May you have enough money and assets to support your church and Christian ministry and comfortably fulfill all the different blessings God has given to you.

Money Blessings Poem

May your pockets flow with coins and your purse flow with cash.
May your savings and investments mount while you work less.
May your bank accounts always be a considerable open stash,
leaving funds to help others and no debts for debtors to address.

May your financial ventures yield a constant positive cash flow.
May you share more and more with nobody to lose.
May you leave yourself more financial donations than you ever thought you would know,
sharing the biggest cash amounts with poor needs to choose.

May you want for nothing and no donation opportunity miss.
May you live comfortably and happily as your family, friends, and needy donations accumulate.
May you have all it takes to afford what brings happiness and bliss,
providing all the good things your family, friends, and needy others can accommodate.

May resources always be ready and near at hand.
May you accumulate enough money to support problems in your blessing roles.
May you fulfill any financial requirement the needy ones may demand,
praying to God to support you in achieving your money blessings goals.

Money Blessings Vision

I manage money well enough to consistently produce a positive cash flow for my family, my friends, and the needs of my blessings projects and ventures. My results leave me more financially secure and satisfied.

My financial management skills have improved to the point that I avoid financial catastrophes. I have enough money available to provide my family and me with the basic necessities and luxuries we need and want.

I possess enough basic assets that allow me to help friends with major problems and to make donations to needy people and organizations. I have improved assets and savings that resulted in me working less and less, producing more and more income and financially supporting my blessings.

I live comfortably and happily myself, while operating within my means. I buy everything I understand to be my basic needs and the basic needs of others.
My basic actions cover basic needs and donations at a level that I never choose to spend it all. I continue to be debtfree.

My new and effective money management approach is leaving mein a better relationship with my family and friends.

My regular prayers with God are helping me to achieve my money blessings goals, involving my family, my friends, my church, its Christian ministry, and the needy.

Money Blessings Process—Daily Action Plan

1. Maximize income sources.
   Examples of things to do: Focus your money blessings. Protect current income sources. Do things to increase current income (become more valuable). Find additional sources of income. Spend no more than you make. Delay gratification until you have the cash for your money blessings.

2. Eliminate debt and wasting money.
   Examples of things to avoid: Neglect desires to get and use your assets in a way that hurts your chances of achieving your money blessings goals. Avoid the use of poor money management skills and behaviors that result in spending more than you earn. Buying things that are not important to your happiness is not productive. Leaving debt unpaid and creating new debt is dangerous, disheartening, and hurtful. Measure the results (net assets and savings) you have achieved by managing your money effectively. Also measure the amount of money you have wasted.

3. Assess how to get good value out of your money management.
   Examples of things to do: Measure the amount of money you save and waste and any credit level you have made.

4. Increase savings and investments.
   Examples of things to do: Establish a regular savings habit. Invest wisely with savings. Leave savings and investments untouched for long periods.

Money Blessings Process—Weekly Action Plan

1. Review your favorite sections in this book.

2. Study the "Money Blessings" sections.
   Examples of things to do: "Money Blessings" statement, poem, vision, and daily action plan.

3. Assess your accomplishments.
   Examples of things to do: Protect your money sources. Increase your income. Add new income sources. Provide some support for your problems. Celebrate your positive accomplishments by yourself or with friends.

4. Address your problems.
   Examples of things to do: Limit spending above your money blessings plan and goals. Delay personal gratification. Avoid waste. Pay off debt.

5. Assess what you've learned.
   Examples of things to ask: What did you accomplish? For example, did you start a savings account, invest well, or leave money untouched except to fund money blessings plans? What improvements in your skills did you achieve? What improvements are needed during the next week?

6. Pray to God.
   Examples of things to do: Thank Him for all the blessings fresh on your mind (including money blessings). Thank Him for your accomplishments. Ask for His support in next week's plan.

Blessed are the merciful, for they shall obtain mercy.
Matthew 5:7 *(Revised Standard Version)*

G
Fun and Adventure Blessings

Fun and Adventure Blessings Statement

May you be blessed with an abundance of funand with every day full of interesting and exciting things to do.

May your life be so much fun and have so much meaningthat you are always eager to get up in the morning and reluctant to go to bed at night.

May you have all the freedom to dowhat you want, how you want to do it, and when you want to do it.

When happy, may the things you do be so exciting and so consumingthat your time seems to race by and you never get caught just wasting your time.

May you love what you do so muchthat you often have a smile on your face while working.May you laugh often and feel a true sense of pride and joy in your work.May you always feel you just can't get enough of lifeand never think of trading jobs or lifestyles with anyone else in the world.

May you never feel depressed, lost, or without direction or purpose, instead, may you feel a real sense of accomplishment and value.May you feel extra fun and adventure by praying often and strongly for it to God.

Fun and Adventure Blessings Poem

May your life be blessed with so much adventure and fun.
May every day be full of interesting and exciting things to do.
May each day you wake up eager to get started and ready to run.
May your time always slip away before you want the day to be through.

May you have all the freedom to do what you want and to win.
May your labors be with family and friends, generating a constant smile.
May no one stand over you, telling you how and when,
producing a true sense of joy in your work all the while.

May you never feel bored, useless, depressed, lost, or blue.
May you be full of blessings and pride.
May you feel a real sense of accomplishment and value,
keeping fun, adventure, and God on your side.

May the glory of your adventures never go completely out of sight.
May you love your life and live it with such fun.
May you never be ready to call it a day and escape to bed at night.
Pray to God to never let you trade jobs or lifestyles with anyone.

Fun and Adventure Blessings Vision

I live with an abundance of fun and adventure.I have lots of interesting and exciting things to do.

I always get up early and go to bed late, with time racing by.I execute fun and adventure blessings action planswithout stopping for other ventures that are not so exciting and consuming.

I love what I do so much that I include fun-loving family and friends with a constant smile on my face.

I work long and hard with frequent laughter and a true sense of pride and joy in my efforts.

I never feel depressed, lost, or without direction or purposebut I am consumed with a real sense of accomplishment and value.

I frequently ask God in prayer for fun and adventure with my family and friends,thanking Him for all my accomplishments and not wanting to trade my job and lifestyle with anyone else in the world.

Fun and Adventure Blessings Process—Daily Action Plan

1. Do meaningful things.
   Examples of things to do: Include things for you (and time spent by you) that are fun, satisfying, supportive of your goals, interesting, exciting, challenging, relaxing, adventurous, and helpful to other people (friends).

2. Avoid doing things that aren't meaningful.
   Examples of things to avoid: Things (and time spent by you) that aren't fun for you, that are dissatisfying, that are boring, that oppose your goals, that waste your time, that drain your energy, that are stressful, and that hurt other people (especially friends).

Fun and Adventure Blessings Process—Weekly Action Plan

1. Review your favorite sections in this book.

2. Study the "Fun and Adventure Blessings" section.
   Examples of things to do: Review "Fun and Adventure Blessings" statement, poem, vision, and daily action plan.

3. Assess your accomplishments.
   Examples of things to measure:
   - the number of (and time spent on) things that are fun, adventurous, challenging, satisfying, supportive of your goals, interesting, exciting, relaxing, and helpful to others;
   - the number of things you do and time spent avoiding things that are not fun, dissatisfying, boring, in opposition to goals, time wasters, energy drains, stress producers, and hurtful to others (friends);
   - the number of things you have done to address your problems;
   - the number of times you have celebrated your positive accomplishments.

4. Assess what you've learned.
   Examples of things to ask: What did you accomplish? What improvements in your skills did you achieve? What improvements are needed for the next week's plan?

5. Pray to God.
   Examples of things to do: Thank Him for the blessings fresh on your mind. Thank Him for your accomplishments. Ask for His support in next week's plan.

Blessed are the pure in heart, for they shall see God.
Matthew 5:8 *(Revised Standard Version)*

H
Religion Blessings

Religion Blessings Statement

God is the source of "Religion Blessings." The Bible is the source for the history and instruction of religion.
See Matthew 5:1–12 and Luke 6:20-23(after "Religion Blessings" vision.)

The Bible includes the definition of the Trinity, which includes God the Father, Jesus the Son, and the Holy Spirit.Being keenly aware of and sensitive to the Trinity helps you receive blessings of all types.

Religion provides meaningful contact with church memberswho likely have been provided as friendship blessings.

You will receive great support in your blessings through church staff and its members.You will greatly support your church-related religion blessings through the church's principles, teachings, worship, support, and love.

You should communicate your religious beliefs to family members, friends, and people you meet.Your ability to achieve goals of religion blessings in a strong, positive way will be of significant value to you and to others.

Religion blessings, when properly addressed, result in good religious plans, goals, actions, and results.When religion blessing goals are set and satisfied, they provide wonderful beliefs and results for you and other people.

Receiving all blessings will be greatly aided by prayer to God. Frequently ask yourself, "What does God want from me?" The answer is provided in the blessings He sends and expects you to address. Your relationship with God depends on how much you respond to and achieve the goals of blessings He transfers to you.

Religion Blessings Poem

God is the center of religion for all.
He provides blessings full of love for His children and more.
His Bible includes important instruction for prayer and call,
providing key principles for your blessings to use as an open door.

Religion provides meaningful contact with the church staff and its members,
Through them you receive great support down here and up above.
You will experience the church's principles, teachings, and worship to remember,
and most of all from your friendships and love.

You should communicate your religious beliefs to all
and share your blessings in a strong, positive way.
Religion can be addressed with clear plans, goals, actions, and results on call,
giving you important things to demonstrate to others every day.

Blessings and results come through your prayers to God each day.
You should often wonder, *What does God really want from me?*
Think through your blessings, and follow the religious ways.
Thoroughly study your blessings, finding what God wants you to be.

Religion Blessings Vision

I am blessed with a great relationship with God.I am accepted by the members and staff of my church.I am in friendship and love with all of them.I read the Bible and learn from it each time I pick it up.

I am open with my religion with everyone I know and meet.I search for blessings everywhere I go.Religion blessings are many and as challenging as any other kind.I frequently succeed in them and am recognized as a good example by my friends and other people.

Praying to God every day provides recognition from Him. He provides more understanding, encouragement,and ideas for giving me more of my blessings.Communicating with God results in improvementsin my commitment and my approaches.Staying focused on my blessings has provided peace and joy and made me more aware of what God wants me to be.

Jesus's Sermon on the Mount (Matthew 5:1-12)

Seeing the crowds, he went up on the mountain, and when he sat down his disciples came to him. And he opened his mouth and taught them saying:

"Blessed are the poor in spirit, for theirs is the kingdom of heaven."

"Blessed are those who mourn, for they shall be comforted.

"Blessed are the meek, for they shall inherit the earth."

"Blessed are they who hunger and thirst for righteousness, for they shall be satisfied."

"Blessed are the merciful, for they shall obtain mercy."

"Blessed are the pure in heart, for they shall see God."

"Blessed are the peacemakers, for they shall be called sons of God."

"Blessed are those who are persecuted for righteousness' sake, for theirs is the kingdom of heaven."

"Blessed are you when men revile you and persecute you and utter all kinds of evil against you falsely on my account. Rejoice and be glad, for your reward is great in heaven, for so men persecuted the prophets who were before you."

Jesus's Sermon to His Disciples and a Multitude of People (Luke 6:20-23)

And He lifted up His eyes on His disciples, and said:

"Blessed are you poor, for yours is the kingdom of God."

"Blessed are you that hunger now, for you shall be satisfied."

"Blessed are you that weep now, for you shall laugh."

"Blessed are you when men hate you, and when they exclude you and revile you, and cast out your name as evil, on account of the Son of man!"

"Rejoice in that day, and leap for joy, for behold, your reward is great in heaven; for so their fathers did to the prophets."

Religion Blessings Process—Daily Action Plan

1. Read the "Religion Blessings" section.
   Examples of things to do: Attend church regularly. Develop proper friendships with members and staff. Obtain knowledge and recognition of the church's blessings. Mentally lay out your plan for achieving the vision today.

2. Contact people in your "Religion Blessings" plan.
   Examples of things to do: Make telephone calls, send emails, write letters, send cards, or visit.

3. Ask how their situation in religion is.
   Examples of things to ask: How are you doing? How much do these ideas mean to you? What's going on in your religious life today that I can help with? Any problems?

4. Provide any support they need.
   Examples of things to do: Make sure you understand your friends' problems. Offer to help however they need support. Make sure you understand their successes. Offer to help celebrate their significant happenings.

5. Look back on your day and evaluate.
   Examples of ways to improve: Assess how much of your "Religious Blessings" plan you have executed today so far. Evaluate how well you have offered to support others. If your plan for helping them is not sufficient, contact them and offer a better plan.

Religious BlessingsProcess—Weekly Action Plan

1. Review your favorite sections in this book.

2. Study the "Religion Blessings" section.
   Examples of things to do: Study "Religion Blessings" statement, poem, vision, and daily action plan.

3. Assess your accomplishments.
   Examples of things to measure and ask: Measure the number/percentage of church members you share love and friendship with. How much did you provide support to your friends? How many meaningful celebrations of your friends' positive accomplishments did you have? Count your blessings and celebrations with them.

4. Assess what you've learned.
   Examples of things to ask: What did you accomplish? Did you learn from your attendance at church and from reading the Bible? What improvements in your skills did you achieve? What do you plan to do next week in this area?

5. Pray to God.
   Examples of things to do: Thank Him for the blessings fresh on your mind. Thank Him for your accomplishments. Ask for His support in next week's plan.

Blessed are the peacemakers, for they shall be called sons of God. Blessed are those who are persecuted for righteousness sake, for theirs is the kingdom of heaven. Matthew 5:9-10 *(Revised Standard Version)*

Chapter 9

HOW MUCH DO YOU GETOUT OF CHRIST JESUS'S BLESSINGS?

I'm glad you made it through this book on blessings. We all can be close to Christ Jesus. We all have His blessings to use and achieve effective Christian achievements. We make mistakes, but we need to backup and successfully ask for forgiveness. He will honor us and cover our important life-style.

Thank you for thinking about and considering the things I covered from Christ Jesus in this book. Christ Jesus led me to do this.

Printed in the USA
CPSIA information can be obtained
at www.ICGtesting.com
LVHW010423110724
785188LV00002B/152